THE GOSPEL UNVEILED

The Gospel Unveiled
Building Disciples by Reealing the Truth of the Gospel

This book is set in the typeface *Athelas* designed by Veronika Burian and Jose Scaglione.

Paperback ISBN: 978-1-967262-44-1

A Publication of *Tall Pine Books*
PO Box 42 Warsaw | Indiana 46581
www.tallpinebooks.com

| 1 26 26 20 16 02 |

Published in the United States of America

THE GOSPEL UNVEILED

BUILDING DISCIPLES BY REVEALING THE TRUTH OF THE GOSPEL

MARISSA BUSBY

Reading *The Gospel Unveiled* felt like sitting with a spiritual mother who loves Jesus deeply and desires to see His children rooted in truth. Marissa takes readers on a journey from creation to redemption with simplicity, depth, and biblical conviction. This book lifts the veil off confusion and brings believers back to the heart of the Gospel—Jesus Himself. It ignites hunger for holiness, intimacy, and spiritual maturity. The reflection sections are especially powerful, offering space for true heart work and Spirit-led transformation. We will be recommending this to new believers, growing believers, and anyone ready to walk in the fullness of God.

Pastors Carlos & Diana Ramirez
New River City Church, Cooper City, Florida

Marissa had a radical encounter with the person of the Holy Spirit as a young woman that led her to give her life away to the broken and to those who don't know the Lord Jesus. We often hear stories like this—and they are all powerful—but in Marissa's case, God did something unique in her life after that encounter. She also fell in love with the written *logos* word of God. She devoured His word and, in doing so, gained a burden to see not only the call to missions fulfilled and the lost saved but also those who have met the Lord Jesus grow in their understanding of Him and be discipled. Marissa has a beautiful hunger for both the "go" of the gospel and the heart to sit with others and see each one discipled in the ways of God. In *The Gospel Unveiled*, she clearly articulates this beautiful story of a loving God saving his lost sons and daughters from Genesis to the cross of Calvary. It clearly and simply answers the questions "Why did Jesus need to come save us?" and "What does salvation look like?" and presents many other simple yet profound foundational truths for our faith. I encourage any believer to read this book and watch as God shores up your foundations of this amazingly good news: the Gospel of Jesus Christ!

Will Hart
CEO, Iris Global

I've known the Lord for over 50 years now, and in that time, I've met very few people who match the passion I see in Marissa (and her husband Sean). Her pursuit of God, her ministry, and her calling are all marked by energy and focus. As I see it, her anointing is in the area of discipleship, and it's a joy to see how, like a magnet, those seeking are drawn to her and she to them. It only makes sense that she would seek to develop the tools needed for that purpose. This book grows out of her passion to disciple those hungry hearts. I highly recommend *The Gospel Unveiled* for anyone on the journey of discipleship, and also those who take seriously the call to "make disciples.

Reverend James Stephen
Elder at *Foundation Church*, Pottstown, PA

The Gospel Unveiled is a clear, compelling, and Spirit-breathed invitation to see Jesus as He truly is. Marissa writes with a rare blend of biblical clarity and prophetic insight, lifting the veil from the Gospel and restoring its power, purity, and beauty. This book awakens identity, calls believers into true sonship, and anchors readers in the finished work of Christ. It's accessible, theologically sound, and deeply stirring. I wholeheartedly recommend it to anyone hungry for a deeper revelation of Jesus and the transformative life of a disciple.

Justin Allen
Founder, *Times and Seasons LLC*
Author, Prophetic Teacher, Trainer, and Equipper

The Gospel Unveiled engages your mind and ignites your heart to embrace and experience the true meaning of the Gospel. The Gospel is the Good News that the LORD Jesus Christ both portrayed and proclaimed. In this book, Marissa does a beautiful job of outlining the way to eternal life and what it means to be a disciple of Jesus. She gives clarity to the question that everyone contemplates about God and His plan of salvation by becoming a follower of Jesus. Every reader will benefit from the solid insights that fill the pages of this book.

Barry Perez
Founder of *Harvestime Ministries Intl.*

The Gospel Unveiled by Marissa Busby is an invaluable resource for everyone with a heart to be a disciple and a disciple maker. Revealing the truth of the Bible from the very first page of the introduction straight through to the conclusion, Marissa builds teaching with application chapter after chapter. She shares biblical truth and life application on a platter, paired with guided reflection and intentional listening. Within the pages of this book, you will quickly see that Jesus is at the epicenter of every sentence. He is the heartbeat of the Gospel, and this book continually points to Him with clarity and care, empowering the reader to learn and then share the Gospel with boldness. Marissa reminds the reader to engage personally with God along the way, asking Jesus to reveal Himself, knowing that He will. Each chapter includes a guided reflection, a powerful tool that reminds readers to align their thoughts and lives with God's truth. The author asks each of us to listen for the Lord's voice and to check what we hear against the plumbline of scripture. As a Christian creative who studies the Bible daily, I found this offering to be a wise and sound resource that will deepen anyone's conviction and understanding of the word of God!

Amanda Schaefer
Global Podcast Host of *A Cup of Gratitude*, Award-winning Author of Six Books, Including *Holy Plot Twists: God is Still Writing Your Story*, and an International Platform Speaker

To my best friend, King, Lord, Savior, and Christ, I dedicate this book. Without Him, I would be nothing, and in Him, I am home. Thank You, Jesus, for the words to speak and the authority to move. I honor You in every word typed here, and I ask You to have Your way with this story.

CONTENTS

Foreword xiii

Introduction xvii

1. Creator and Creation 1
    Chapter One Reflection 9
2. Dominion 13
    Chapter Two Reflection 23
3. A Covering 27
    Chapter Three Reflection 35
4. Definition and Decisions 39
    Chapter Four Reflection 47
5. Born Again 51
    Chapter Five Reflection 65
6. Justification and Sanctification 69
    Chapter Six Reflection 80
7. Pure in Heart 83
    Chapter Seven Reflection 92
8. Holy Spirit 95
    Chapter Eight Reflection 102
9. Kingdom Culture 105
    Chapter Nine Reflection 113

Conclusion 117

Acknowledgements 121

About the Author 125

FOREWORD

I believe with all my heart that we are on the brink of a discipleship movement in the body of Christ. We are witnessing a tremendous influx of people giving their hearts to the Lord. These precious people can't be left as they are; they need discipleship. After all, God desires that orphans would come to know that they are sons and daughters of God—there is a Father who loves them. He then wants to mature them to rise as fathers and mothers, that they may lead wherever He has called them. This is why books like *The Gospel Unveiled* by Marissa Busby are a gift to the church.

We live in a time where teachers and teaching are plentiful, but that doesn't mean that all are safe. Currently, many opinions that aren't biblical are being broadcast as doctrine. Secondary and tertiary theology has taken center stage in many people's attention. Meanwhile, the Spirit of God is pointing the church back to the simplicity of the gospel. He is emphasizing how our foundation needs to be priority.

The Spirit of God is pointing us back to our primary doctrine: Jesus.

I found myself refreshed as I read through each chapter of *The Gospel Unveiled*. Marissa's purity of heart and love are evident in her writing, and I found myself encouraged by the words of someone who, no doubt, has allowed her roots to delve deep into the love of Jesus. I believe that those who read her words will feel greatly cared for and pastored. There is no doubt in my mind that this book will help to lay a healthy biblical foundation for those who pick it up. I am thankful that the Lord has raised voices like Marissa to train and equip the body of Christ.

As I've had the honor of serving churches throughout the world, I've observed an important truth. The long-term success of a ministry isn't determined by gifting, although gifting is unarguably important. The legacy of a church isn't guaranteed by reach and influence. Longevity and legacy are determined by the health of a foundation. A healthy foundation is forged through unwavering friendship with Jesus. This is why I believe books, like the one in your hands, are so important. *The Gospel Unveiled* is a roadmap to spiritual health.

As you read this book, I encourage you to open your heart. Let Him move you. Let God root you deeply. *The Gospel Unveiled* is an invitation into the wonderful heart of Jesus.

Dr. Luc Niebergall
Prophetic Voice & Author

INTRODUCTION

[Jesus] said to them, "Go into all the world and preach the gospel to all creation," (Matthew 16:15 NIV).

This is the mandate for all Christians: preach the Gospel. Yet, many are confused about what the Gospel even is. The rhetoric stating, "Simply invite Jesus into your heart, and you will go to Heaven," floats around religious circles with little substance. It begs the question, "Who is this God I am asked to dedicate my life to? Who is this Jesus that is so widely debated?"

To preach that which comes from Him, we must first *know* Him.

Even to this day when Moses is read, a veil covers their hearts. But whenever anyone turns to the Lord,

> *the veil is taken away. Now the Lord is the Spirit, and where the Spirit of the Lord is, there is freedom. And we all, who with unveiled faces contemplate the Lord's glory, are being transformed into His image with ever-increasing glory, which comes from the Lord, who is the Spirit (2 Corinthians 3:15-18 NIV).*

The heartbeat of the Gospel revolves around Jesus, the Lord. Without Him, the veil remains, covering hearts and making it impossible to see and comprehend the glory of God. But my prayer as we journey through these pages together is this: Those who have eyes, let them see. Those who have ears, let them hear.

This story is meant to unveil the person of Jesus so that the Gospel may be known with clarity, giving us the ability to share it with boldness. Relationship with God is possible through the revelation of Jesus alone, because through Him we are called children of God. The earth is groaning for the awakening of sons and daughters—for a deep declaration of family. There is a call to disciple in this season: to know God and make Him known. Disciples are created through the unveiling of the Gospel, which reveals that friendship with God is not just a possibility but the very heart and essence of the Father.

As you turn these pages, take a deep breath and ask Jesus to reveal Himself to you. May a great unveiling take place as you dig into God's story, which, in turn, has become your story. This is not a book meant to be read; it's a book to be devoured, designed to ignite a fire in your bones and inspire you to live out your calling and purpose on this earth.

Jesus is beautiful, radiant, full of glory, worthy of all praise, the Name above all other names. The greatest work you will ever do is getting to *know* your Savior and Lord. Let us unveil this King of all kings, this Lamb of God slain for the sins of man. Here stands the unveiled Gospel.

CHAPTER ONE

Creator and Creation

In the beginning God created the heavens and the earth. The earth was without form and void, and darkness was over the face of the deep. And the Spirit of God was hovering over the face of the waters. God said, "Let there be light," and there was light (Genesis 1:1–3 ESV).

The heart of the Gospel starts at the very beginning of time, when "darkness covered the face of the deep." This verse resonates deeply with my spirit each time I read Genesis because it reveals the very nature of God: He is faithful to never leave us in darkness. There Holy Spirit was, in the very beginning, hovering over the face of the waters—waiting, watching, and getting ready to move. He brought light to dark places. He brought abundance to what was previously empty. He brought life through His very breath. If we want to know the nature of God, we must go to the start.

Let me set the stage. The world is dark, empty, and void. There is nothing in existence, yet God is there. He is Alpha and Omega: the beginning and the end. We struggle to comprehend this because, as long as we have been, there has been. Time started for humanity the moment God created humanity, but before that, time was non-existent, completely obsolete, and simply unnecessary. God is not limited by a time domain, and His presence is not contained within it.

Often, we evaluate human behavior through the lens of nature and nurture. "Were they born this way or were they made to be this way?" This is not a question we can ask about God since He existed before all things. He cannot be nurtured into something different because His nature is unchanging, established before the foundation of time. That is a wild thought, and it is hard to wrap our human minds around. He is outside of time, but He must be.

The Creator of all things must exist before the creation of all things; He is the uncreated One. What came first, the chicken or the egg? This is a funny little argument we have all discussed at some point, but the truth is, both answers are incorrect. The Creator came first so He could create the chicken. He is before all things, in all things, and is the finisher of all things. He is the Maker of all that is good and the Master of the skies and seas. His plan was union with His creation. Yet, we cannot see evidence of this design when we look at the world today. We see darkness, death, and destruction. We observe chaos and crisis—children starving, natural disasters, political discord, sexual sin and abuse, and rebellion.

How often do we find ourselves asking, "If God is truly good, why did this happen?" The reality of this present darkness is that it clouds out the goodness of God if we do not understand the ultimate design. His nature may seem cruel when we view Him through the lens of what we see with earthly eyes. We are left unable to understand how a loving God could allow such suffering to His creation. But what if the darkness we often see was never part of His original plan? What if His plan was always rooted in goodness, mercy, justice, grace, love, peace, and union with His creation? I am here to tell you that, no matter how hard it might be to believe, this truth remains: His design was good from the very beginning.

Love Multiplied

> *Then God said, "Let us make man in our image, after our likeness. And let them have dominion over the fish of the sea and over the birds of the heavens and over the livestock and over all the earth and over every creeping thing that creeps on the earth."*
>
> *So God created man in his own image, in the image of God he created him; male and female he created them (Genesis 1:26-27 ESV).*

Just as we saw the heart of God from the very beginning, we also see His plan: a relationship with those He created. Humanity is the pinnacle of creation, the only life given through the breath of God. For all the animals, land, water, skies, and seas, God said, "Let it be so," and it was. And He found it good. When He made Adam, He breathed His breath into him. Then, He took a rib from Adam's side to create Eve. God created male and female in His image, and He walked with them in the cool of the Garden. I am wrecked by this fact—that the Creator of all things would choose to walk, talk, and be with His creation. His goodness and mercy are endlessly evident in this truth.

From the beginning, the One who created everything has existed as the Trinity—one God in three persons. Now, how can this be? How can God be the Father, the Son, and the Spirit, and yet they are all unique and distinct? There are Bible scholars who have spent their life's work studying and trying to communicate an understanding of the Trinity. The concept of the Godhead being three in one is complex, and it is something I do not fully understand nor can adequately describe. The point I want you to hear is that we are not meant to fully understand everything about God. The finite mind cannot comprehend an infinite God, and we must not base our theology on what we can understand in fullness.

If we knew every aspect of all things pertaining to the Godhead, there would be no need for Holy Spirit to bring us revelation of the mysteries of the Gospel. Part of our relationship as creation with Creator God is to trust in faith and walk without perfect sight. As I write this, I pray you are asking Holy Spirit to reveal these hidden mysteries to your heart—that your eyes would be opened to new clarity of what God is doing in you and what He has done for you. We *need* Him in order to *know* Him, and we will spend the rest of eternity unearthing the different facets of God.

To pursue Him, share the Gospel, and bring glory to His name effectively and without confusion or disorder, we must know His role and our role and stay in our lane. He is God; we are not. He is above and beyond our comprehension, and it is beautiful. I rejoice in this fact. I don't know everything, and I praise the good Lord for that. He does His job far, far, FAR better than I ever could, so I will honor Him by allowing concepts of Him to be outside my reach. I will worship Him through my ability to submit to Him in faith, even when I don't understand completely.

And yet, we are not blind mice trying to scamper our way through a maze to find cheese; the Lord gives us revelation through His Spirit; what a wonderful gift! He is God; we are not, and yet in His infinite mercy, He does not leave us orphans, without a home and without understanding. He sent us the gift of Holy Spirit to reveal of the mysteries of the Gospel, and the Bible says we carry these mysteries through Him. 1 Corinthians 4:1 states, *"This is how one should regard us, as servants of Christ and stewards of the mysteries of God"* (ESV). You, my friend, steward the mysteries of God; the key word here being *steward*. We have a responsibility to carry what the Spirit reveals to us and to release what we do not yet know, walking in faith. He will give us revelation as we ask.

That said, let me try to explain the concept of the Trinity as best as I can. God said, "Let *us* make man in *our* image." God Himself is plural. This is not some gender pronoun situation the Lord is working through; this is His identity. He is God the Father. Jesus is the Son. Holy Spirit is the manifest Spirit of God. There are three distinct persons, yet they form the same one. A common analogy of this is an egg. An egg has a shell, a white part, and a yolk. Each part is separate with its own qualities and purpose, yet they are all needed to form the entire egg. Another great analogy my husband teaches in men's discipleship is the sun. The sun itself is like Father God, who is the source of all life. The light we see is like Jesus the Son, who is the radiance of glory that reveals the heart of the Father. And the heat we feel from the sun is like Holy Spirit, who is the tangible presence that is with us and changes us. I love these analogies, but I feel they miss the *why* behind the fact that God is three.

When a husband and wife join in marriage, children are often a byproduct. I am not going to get all weird on you guys and have a sex talk here, but I do want to note how when two become one in marriage, they generally want to multiply their love forward. Children are love multiplied. This is similar to how I see the Trinity.

God is love. The Bible does not say God acts out love; it says He *is* love. And He is so deeply full of love that it must multiply. It is wave upon wave, crashing its glory on the shores of despair, washing away all that once was and leaving beauty in its place. It is a roaring fire, growing exponentially as it rips through the forest, pulling everything into its embrace. Love desperately wants to expand. It wants to be poured out on new life, new creation, multiplied forward, and expanded. God, Jesus, and Holy Spirit are the definition of true love, spiraling and circling in a whirlwind of life. Love must multiply.

So, why did God create? Because He is love and love must pour over. It cannot be contained, and it wants to flow through every crevasse, filling every crack and laying a deep foundation of connection. Love multiplies, so God said, "Let us make man in our image." You, my friend, are the love of God multiplied out on this earth for all to see, deeply and wholly loved by the Creator Himself.

CHAPTER ONE REFLECTION

Take 15–30 minutes to do this section; do not rush what the Lord is going to teach you during your time with Him. Before you jump to the questions, stop and ask God to speak to you. Ask Him to fill you with understanding and reveal His heart for you.

God's design has always been relationship with creation. Do you have a personal relationship with God? If yes, how is it? If not, what do you feel is holding you back?

Have you ever found yourself asking the question, "If God is good, why did this happen?" Is it hard for you to reconcile that His plan never intended for the evil you've experienced? Take some time to share your honest thoughts with God and ask Him to reveal His goodness to you. Ask Him to help you be okay with not having perfect answers to these questions.

Do you believe that you are loved by God? I am here to tell you that you are. But, if you do not believe this, take a minute to write to the Lord why you feel the way you feel. If you do believe this, tell Him thank you.

This is the most crucial step, which we will repeat at the end of every chapter. I want you to ask the Lord to speak to you and you to listen. You can hear Him. He speaks to our hearts, through His Word, in images in our minds (because a picture is worth a thousand words), through other people, audibly, and in any other way He wants. Take 10 minutes to sit quietly. Ask God to speak to you about this chapter and believe that He will. Write down what you are asking Him and then write His reply. Here are two ways to evaluate if it is a word from God.

Does it line up with His Word? He will never contradict the Bible.

Is it spoken in love? Even His discipline is bathed with love and draws us close. It does not push us away in anxiety and chaos.

CHAPTER TWO

Dominion

Now we see that love was multiplied and poured out from the breath of God when He created Adam. Then, from his side, a rib was taken, and Eve was formed because, again, the Kingdom is to be expanded. Adam could have ruled over the animals and the Garden, but he did not have the ability to multiply or expand without a woman to create life with. Their union and creation are testaments to the love of the Trinity. So, the Creator made them male and female, partners for the good of the earth and the glory of the Kingdom.

Adam and Eve spent their days working in the Garden of Eden. They were given dominion over it and commanded by the Lord to name the animals and tend the ground. Because God created the world, He had full authority over it. However, He grants Adam and Eve dominion to reign and rule; He sets them up as "His right hands," if you will, to serve as examples of His love and Kingdom in that place. They had authority over the Garden of Eden because God Himself commissioned them. God said in Genesis 1:28, "...*'Be fruitful and multiply and fill the earth and subdue it, and have dominion over the fish of the sea and over the birds of the heavens and over every living thing that moves on the earth'*" (ESV). Adam and Eve were called to take the peace they found in the Garden, multiply it across the earth, and push back the powers of the adversary who was roaming like a lion, looking to devour any prey he could find.

So...who is this adversary?

Because God is holy and worthy of all honor, a host of angels constantly poured out their praise to Him and moved at His word. That is, until one of these angels had a shift of heart and no longer wanted to worship God. He became the living, breathing definition of pride, marking our first Biblical encounter with what happens when someone, or something, loses focus on God and His majesty and instead focuses on himself and his "truth."

His eyes went inward instead of upward on God, and it became all about him and what he felt and wanted. Anger and bitterness ruled him as he sought the glory and praise for himself. This angel wanted to be like God; in fact, he wished to *be* God. Pride oozed from him as he demanded to have the throne to himself. This angel is who we now know to be Satan, and he was cast down from Heaven by God Himself.

> *How you have fallen from heaven, morning star, son of the dawn! You have been cast down to the earth, you who once laid low the nations! You said in your heart, "I will ascend to the heavens; I will raise my throne above the stars of God; I will sit enthroned on the mount of assembly, on the utmost heights of Mount Zaphon. I will ascend above the tops of the clouds; I will make myself like the Most High." But you are brought down to the realm of the dead, to the depths of the pit (Isaiah 14:12–15 NIV).*

The most High God, the King of the universe, is definitely not one to tolerate pride. Pride is sin, and sin leads to death, which is ultimately separation from God. And that is precisely what happened to Satan—separation.

You see, sin and holiness could not coexist because they are polar opposites. A magnet is attracted to another magnet, but if you turn one around, it repels the other, no matter what you do. God and pride were like these magnets—they could not dwell in the same space, competing for the same throne, because that throne belongs to God alone. Satan had two choices: turn back to God, repent, and acknowledge Him as the Most High, or leave. Pride chose pride, setting his sights on war with God, and God cast him from the heavens, sending him to roam the earth with all the fallen angels that chose to follow him and place pride above the holiness of God.

Now, Satan is roaming the earth, full of hatred of God, set on destroying all God is and loves so that he may inhabit the throne. When God created man and woman, His call to be fruitful and multiply was not simply about having babies and keeping humanity alive. It was a call to take their God-given dominion and authority over the powers of darkness that roar; to push back the workings of pride and to expand the glory of God. The enemy's rule stood no chance because the very breath of God is what brought life to humanity. Authority was theirs because God commanded them to go, and God dwelt with them in the Garden.

Now, that same authority has been given to us if we choose relationship with God and know Whose breath we house.

The Fall

Up to this point in the story, the plan for Adam and Eve was beautiful: they were meant to dwell with God, have dominion over the earth, and spread the Kingdom far and wide as they walked in relationship with Him. However, for creation to have a relationship with the Creator, there must be free will. Satan himself, as an angel, had free will to worship God or worship himself. Man must also have a choice to walk with *or* apart from God. Love multiplied is not true love if it is forced, manipulated, or gaslighted.

Take my husband and me, for example. If I were forced to be at our wedding and not allowed to leave, manipulated into giving myself to him, that would not be love. People go to jail for this sort of thing, and we see many justice workers fighting to eradicate child marriages, forced relationships, and all kinds of abuse around the world. We know these scenarios are wrong, yet we struggle to understand why God would give us free will to disobey Him. He had to. He is love, and love does not insist on its own way.

Love is also firm in boundaries. The holiness of God is not something to play with—we saw Satan attempt this, and he was cast from the heavens. Perfection demanded perfection. There are consequences when we actively choose to disobey God. However, these consequences are not the result of an evil God wanting to punish us; rather, they are evidence of His kindness and grace, which lead us to repentance. The plan He created from the beginning was perfect. It aimed to expand the Kingdom and also considered the good of humanity. The boundaries God established were for humanity's benefit, not to hide, manipulate, or torment them.

I think of the joy I found as a kid going to a theme park and getting ready to sit on the biggest roller coaster I could find. My body was filled with excitement, but I still had nervous butterflies in my stomach as I admired the loops, twists, quick corners, and big drops. When I strapped that seatbelt and safety bar into place and heard it click, I breathed a sigh of relief. I was safe; I was ready.

This roller coaster is much like the journey of life, full of highs and lows, turns and drops, and loops. The boundaries given by God are the rules and regulations, and the standards of the Kingdom are the safety bar. We are strapped in by His kindness and love, ready and secure for every turn. His boundaries are not out of malice or ill intent; rather, they are drenched in love and security. Love also echoes that the choice must be the riders if they want to secure their seatbelt and use the safety bar the Lord has provided. The choice was Adam and Eve's, and the choice is still ours today.

We see this in Genesis 2:15–17:

> *"The Lord God took the man and put him in the garden of Eden to work it and keep it. And the Lord God commanded the man, saying, 'You may surely eat of every tree of the garden, but of the tree of the knowledge of good and evil you shall not eat, for in the day that you eat of it you shall surely die'" (ESV).*

The choice of obedience in faith unto God is there, and the consequence of said choice is clearly spelled out.

There is an argument floating around that the deceiver is actually the good guy in this tale. This argument believes that when he comes to tempt Eve to eat of the tree of the knowledge of good and evil, he is inviting her to have knowledge, and knowledge is power, so God must be the bad guy if He is keeping knowledge from humanity. Wow. I struggle to put words to this type of deception. I am simply reminded of the verse in Isaiah 5:20 ESV that says, *"Woe to those who call evil good and good evil, who put darkness for light and light for darkness, who put bitter for sweet and sweet for bitter!"* This type of deception is a very real thing, and it started with the voice of the adversary in Genesis.

> *Now the serpent was more crafty than any other beast of the field that the Lord God had made. He said to the woman, "Did God actually say, 'You shall not eat of any tree in the garden'?" And the woman said to the serpent, "We may eat of the fruit of the trees in the garden, but God said, 'You shall not eat of the fruit of the tree that is in the midst of the garden, neither shall you touch it, lest you die.'" But the serpent said to the woman, "You will not surely die. For God knows that when you eat of it your eyes will be opened, and you will be like God, knowing good and evil." So, when the woman saw that the tree was good for food, and that it was a delight to the eyes, and that the tree was to be desired to make one wise, she took of its fruit and ate, and she also gave some to her husband who was with her, and he ate. Then the eyes of both were opened, and they knew that they were naked. And they sewed fig leaves together and made themselves loincloths (Genesis 3:1-7 ESV).*

How often do we still hear that familiar voice today? "Did God really say He loves me? Did God really say He is good? Does God really care?" The voice of the enemy remains the same because he cannot create anything new. Remember, the Creator exists outside of creation. Satan cannot create; he can only mimic and distort. His goal is to steal, kill, and destroy, and what he cannot destroy, he manipulates and distorts, planting seeds of doubt and questions in us. When these seeds are allowed to take root, destruction seeps into our actions. But whether we partner with that distortion is up to us. I know that sometimes life throws terrible circumstances our way. I understand that trauma inflicted on us is not a result of what we did but often stems from the sins of others. However, when lies creep in, we must take responsibility for how we choose to partner with them. Lies hold no power until we plant them deep in our hearts. They have no weight until we hand over the authority. The voice is loud and clear: "Did God really say...."

It was a dark moment in the Garden of Eden when deception took root, and the fruit of disobedience led to sin. Sin sprang up like a mature weed, choking out the life Adam and Eve once knew. Its roots were wild and strong, and no matter what they did, they lacked the power or authority to remove them. The deed was done; sin had already entered. Actions lead to consequences, and this was the reality Adam and Eve faced. Sin created an instant divide between the Creator and His creation. They hid from the Lord as He walked into the Garden that day. Deception shouted loudly as creation hid in the shadows, afraid of what was to come.

Deception will run rampant until the end of the age. *"You will not surely die. For God knows that when you eat of it your eyes will be opened, and you will be like God, knowing good and evil."* What a line. This is the one that still deceives many today. It says, "You can be like God. Find your own truth. Live your own life." It is the same voice of the deceiver that we see during our introduction to him in Genesis 3.

Knowledge is viewed as power, so we believe that the more we know, the mightier we are. However, God did not ask Adam and Eve to understand the knowledge of good and evil; He asked for obedience and faith. He asked them to trust Him to have their best in mind; He asked for full faith without full understanding. This, my friend, is what He longs for today: faith even when we do not understand. Faith to say, "You are my God, and I will trust You." He asks for a pursuit of holiness, deep, unadulterated obedience, and submission to Him, and in return, we receive His authority and dominion.

CHAPTER TWO REFLECTION

Take 15-30 minutes to do this section; do not rush what the Lord is going to teach you during your time with Him. Before you jump to the questions, stop and ask God to speak to you. Ask Him to fill you with understanding and reveal His heart for you.

Are you strapped into the "roller coaster of life" with the seatbelt provided by God, or are you continuing to rebel against His design and structure? Are you willing to give your sin and rebellion to Him? If so, what are some areas you can lay down for the Lord?

Adam and Eve hid in the Garden because of shame. Are there areas you are hiding from others, yourself, or even God? Can you be bold enough to reveal them to the Father today?

Adam and Eve were given dominion and authority to expand God's Kingdom. Are you walking in authority and faith? If not, why do you feel you are not?

Take 10 minutes to sit quietly and ask God to speak to you about this chapter. Believe that He will. Write down what you are asking Him and then write His reply.

CHAPTER THREE

A Covering

I like to imagine the next scene in the story as something like this: the footsteps of God echoed like thunder as He walked calmly into the Garden. In reality, His steps probably weren't any louder than they had been in the days prior, but to Adam and Eve, hidden behind the bushes, they were booming with authority. Their hearts trembled with fear and reverence because they saw their nakedness and hid from Him. I can almost visualize tears streaming down Eve's face as the weight of what they had done hit her again, while Adam shivered as he reached out and felt the firm wall that now stood between him and his greatest love, the Creator.

> *The Lord God called to the man and said to him, "Where are you?" And he said, "I heard the sound of you in the garden, and I was afraid, because I was naked, and I hid myself." He said, "Who told you that you were naked? Have you eaten of the tree of which I commanded you not to eat?" The man said, "The woman whom you gave to be with me, she gave me fruit of the tree, and I ate." Then the Lord God said to the woman, "What is this that you have done?" The woman said, "The serpent deceived me, and I ate" (Genesis 3:9–13 ESV).*

There is so much weight in this passage. *"Who told you that you were naked?"* We see right here that God never intended for man to see his nakedness; God never intended for creation to feel or be disconnected from their Creator. Man was naked long before he ever saw his nakedness, yet the heart of God was to protect man from the knowledge of good and evil. The reality of our nakedness has never changed, but under the umbrella of the love of God, and the faith of humanity in Him who is above and beyond us, we were covered. When Adam and Eve sinned, their eyes were opened, and they were left vulnerable, able to see that which God had never intended for them to see. Now, they felt exposed.

Adam and Eve had tried to make loincloths out of fig leaves, but it was not sufficient to cover the shame they now felt, so they hid. How often do we try to fix things in our own strength and realize, rather quickly, how weak we truly are? The work of man is never enough to cover the shame and nakedness humanity carries as a result of sin. We cannot hide, cover up, or redeem that which we have broken.

But God can.

Genesis 3:21 says, *"And the Lord God made for Adam and for his wife garments of skins and clothed them"* (ESV). Up until this point, the Bible does not refer to animal sacrifice. There was no death found in the Garden. But God made garments for them from *animal skins*. Blood was shed to clothe and cover the naked shame of man because it was now required to restore rightness with the Lord. This is not because God demanded blood sacrifice from the beginning, but because skins were needed to cover humanity. But it was only temporary. A covering is only enough for the sin of humanity if it is provided by God Himself. This verse is setting the stage for the coming of Christ, the one covering sufficient to atone for sin completely.

The first set of skins made and provided by God begins the line of animal sacrifice that we see throughout the Old Testament law, an offering for sin so that we could dwell in the presence of God, clothed and covered. Sin and holiness could not coincide; remember the repelling magnets when Satan fought for the throne of God? This theme is echoed here as Adam and Eve listened to the voice of pride over the voice of God. Their eyes were opened to what they were never meant to see, and they were full of shame, which pushed them from the loving heart of God the Father. This temporary sacrifice of skins given by God allowed them the gift of His presence again. But God had an even greater plan for eternal redemption.

> *Indeed, under the law almost everything is purified with blood, and without the shedding of blood there is no forgiveness of sins. Thus, it was necessary for the copies of the heavenly things to be purified with these rites, but the heavenly things themselves with better sacrifices than these. For Christ has entered, not into holy places made with hands, which are copies of the true things, but into heaven itself, now to appear in the presence of God on our behalf. Nor was it to offer himself repeatedly, as the high priest enters the holy*

> *places every year with blood not his own, for then he would have had to suffer repeatedly since the foundation of the world. But as it is, he has appeared once for all at the end of the ages to put away sin by the sacrifice of himself. And just as it is appointed for man to die once, and after that comes judgment, so Christ, having been offered once to bear the sins of many, will appear a second time, not to deal with sin but to save those who are eagerly waiting for him (Hebrews 9:22–28 ESV).*

In the Garden, we see the foreshadowing of the ultimate covering to come: the great high priest, Jesus Christ. But we also see the *need* for a savior like Him.

Judgment and Mercy

The tree of life was planted long before Adam and Eve ate of the tree of the knowledge of good and evil. The plan was always for eternal life in connection with God. However, redemption became necessary to restore mankind to right standing with the Creator, so they could eat of the tree of life again—this time, in union with Him. Thankfully, the person of Jesus, who is redemption and life Himself, has existed from the very beginning of time. The seed of redemption had already taken root. God, in

His great mercy and judgment, established a plan before the creation of man, knowing what was to come. His love, overflowing and multiplying forward, did not allow Him to turn His back on humanity in their fall; instead, He initiated the process of eternal salvation and perfect alignment once more. To do so, He opened up His mouth and cast them from the Garden.

> *Then the Lord God said, "Behold, the man has become like one of us in knowing good and evil. Now, lest he reach out his hand and take also of the tree of life and eat and live forever—" therefore the Lord God sent him out from the garden of Eden to work the ground from which he was taken. He drove out the man, and at the east of the garden of Eden he placed the cherubim and a flaming sword that turned every way to guard the way to the tree of life (Genesis 3:22–24 ESV).*

It is the abundant grace of God that Adam and Eve were cast out of the Garden of Eden. We often think of judgment as harsh or something negative, but here we see it is the deep mercy of God, rooted in true love for humanity. Had they been allowed to stay in the Garden, they would have continued to eat from the tree of life, forever separated from God. Jesus would not have been able to be born of a woman, fulfilling prophecy, and dying for our sins. Prophecy would not have even been established in the first place! Satan would have been able to continue his reign and rule on the earth while man lived far from God. It is God's outstanding grace and mercy that Adam and Eve were cast out because full redemption was only possible when full separation was established.

Looking back to the original plan, we cannot have dominion and multiply the Kingdom of God if we are disconnected from Him. So, He expelled Adam and Eve from the Garden in order for connection to be restored. He sent Jesus to die for the sins of humanity and bring creation and Creator back into union, defeating the kingdom of darkness by descending into the grave and rising again, conquering death completely. Judgment, rooted in deep mercy, set the stage for pure redemption, restoration in union with God, and the defeat of the adversary once and for all.

Just as the kindness of God leads us to repentance, it was the kind judgment of God that brought punishment upon Adam and Eve for their sin, so that they might be redeemed. When you feel as if you are too far gone, wrestling with sin and shame, remember, dear one, that the seed of redemption and restoration was planted long before you took your first breath. The God of the universe saw you, knew your sin, and planned for the redemption of humanity from the very beginning. He still chose to create; He still chose to redeem. He still chooses life, and He still chooses you.

There is no way we can dig ourselves out of the pit created through the act of sin. Yet, there is One, fully God and fully man, who comes to redeem and restore, revealing the heart of the Father to those who have ears to listen and eyes to see. Redemption is available, but it is only found through the person of Jesus. He was with God in the beginning, and through Him, all things were made.

> *In the beginning was the Word, and the Word was with God, and the Word was God. He was with God in the beginning. Through Him all things were made; without Him nothing was made that has been made. In Him was life, and that life was the light of all mankind. The light shines in the darkness, and the darkness has not overcome it (John 1:1-5 ESV).*

CHAPTER THREE REFLECTION

Take 15-30 minutes to do this section; do not rush what the Lord is going to teach you during your time with Him. Before you jump to the questions, stop and ask God to speak to you. Ask Him to fill you with understanding and reveal His heart for you.

How do you perceive that God looks at you? Are you feeling shame for anything, and if so, are you willing to accept His grace and covering?

Fig leaves were not enough to cover the sin and shame of humanity. Have you made "coverings" for yourself to justify actions and sins? If so, what are they?

____

____

____

____

____

____

God casts Adam and Eve out of the Garden of Eden. Many people see it as harsh judgment, but it was pure mercy and love. Is there an area in your life where you have felt God has been harsh? Reflect on that and ask Him where His mercy shines in that situation.

____

____

____

____

____

____

Take 10 minutes to sit quietly and ask God to speak to you about this chapter. Believe that He will. Write down what you are asking Him, and then write His reply.

CHAPTER FOUR

Definition and Decisions

So far, we have established a foundation: the Gospel begins at the beginning, God is the Creator of all things, existing completely outside of time—He is the same yesterday, today, and forever, and His message has never changed. We have also learned that He is three in one, love poured out and multiplied for all to see. And most recently, we have seen that sin entered the world through Adam and Eve, giving us a need for a Savior.

Now, I want to dive a little deeper. How do we define the Gospel? What is this thing we are commanded to do, live out, and share with those around us? What makes it a story worth telling and giving our lives for? The Gospel is quite basic, yet entirely complex. We have a history of overcomplicating it, so I want to make it as simple as I can. The definition of *Gospel* is "good news." And the following is very, very good news indeed.

God created humanity with free will. They could eat fruit from any tree except one: the tree of the knowledge of good and evil. Humanity sinned by eating from this tree, stepping away from the glory of God, and revealing their desperate need for redemption. God, in His grace, mercy, and judgment, saw humanity in their sin and shame, and sent His Son, Jesus. Jesus, fully God and fully man, lived a perfect life. But He ultimately chose to submit to the will of the Father by dying to take our sin upon Himself. Then, three days later, He conquered death by rising from the grave. He took what should have been our eternal demise and wore it on Himself, reconnecting humanity to God.

Now, here is the heart of the Gospel: Anyone who believes in their heart and confesses with their mouth that Jesus is Lord is saved from this eternal separation from God. When God looks at them, He does not see their sin and shame; He sees them through the blood of Jesus. Those who believe and receive this free gift may enter the presence of God boldly because of what Jesus has done. This message is transformative.

This is the Gospel: that while we were still sinners, Jesus saw us and died in our place, freeing us from the bondage of sin.

Simple, right? But it still takes incredible faith to believe.

A question often brought to me is, "How could a good God send people to hell?" Here is the thing: we have already established that God is not the one who desires to send anyone to hell. The Creator's plan was, and is, and always will be union with humanity—walking in the Garden of Eden, communing together, and creating family. The disobedience of humanity is what set us on the path to hell and eternal separation from the Lord. It is *not* the will of God that any should perish. Don't believe me? He says it far better than I can.

> *The Lord is not slow in keeping his promise, as some understand slowness. Instead, he is patient with you, not wanting anyone to perish, but everyone to come to repentance.*
>
> *But the day of the Lord will come like a thief. The heavens will disappear with a roar; the elements will be destroyed by fire, and the earth and everything done in it will be laid bare.*
>
> *Since everything will be destroyed in this way, what kind of people ought you to be? You ought to*

> *live holy and godly lives as you look forward to the day of God and speed its coming. That day will bring about the destruction of the heavens by fire, and the elements will melt in the heat. But in keeping with his promise we are looking forward to a new heaven and a new earth, where righteousness dwells. (2 Peter 3:9–13 NIV)*

> *For God so loved the world, that he gave his only Son, that whoever believes in him should not perish but have eternal life. For God did not send his Son into the world to condemn the world, but in order that the world might be saved through him. (John 3:16–17 ESV)*

The opportunity to strap in with the safety belt on this roller coaster is available to everyone. The option to choose Heaven, which is only found through the gate that is Christ Jesus, is now open to all. We are called to the heart of God, to know Him deeply, love Him eternally, and submit to Him wholeheartedly. We are made to bear His image, a light for the Kingdom shining in dark places, leading others to reconciliation with God. We are called to lead people to the King of kings, to "feed the sheep" and introduce them to the Shepherd. The Gospel is all about what Jesus has done for humanity, and the invitation is open to all who believe and turn to Him.

The Gospel is not really about us. In fact, it has nothing to do with us. The Gospel is past tense. His death and resurrection are a finished work—period. It has everything to do with *His* life, sacrifice, and redemption. Often, I see people come to God for what He can give them. They long for His gifts and blessings or fear going to hell. Yet we see the true Gospel being about what Jesus *has* done, not what we *will* get from Him. *While we were yet sinners*, Christ died for us. Past tense.

While I was buried in my sin and shame, the King of the universe came and gave Himself as a living sacrifice for me, putting an end to death and obliterating all warrants the enemy had out for me. He took the keys to my eternal prison and opened the doors to freedom! He broke my chains, set me free, and gave me life. So, you see, the Gospel is not about me, but rather it is about all that Jesus *has* done, and yet, it *is* all about me in the eyes of God.

God saw us, and He sent Jesus. That sentence right there is enough to end this book. God saw us. Oh, that the King of the universe would even look on me gives me chills. He could have ended humanity after Adam and Eve ate of the tree of the knowledge of good and evil. He could have said, "This is not worth my time." But He chose to give Himself as a sacrifice—He chose to see. And yet, not only does He look our way, but He also gave Himself as our redemption. This is the Gospel.

We see this beautifully laid out in the book of Romans. Many people refer to this as the Romans Road to Salvation. It is a clear set of verses that perfectly depicts the Gospel message, and it is a tool I use to walk new believers into an understanding of salvation. Here is a quick list:

1. Romans 3:23 NIV: "For all have sinned and fall short of the glory of God."

Meaning: We are all sinners. No one is "good enough" for Heaven.

2. Romans 6:23 KJV: "For the wages of sin is death; but the gift of God is eternal life through Jesus Christ our Lord."

Meaning: Sin results in death. Yet, God gave the gift of Jesus to bring us eternal life.

3. Romans 5:8 NIV: "But God demonstrates His own love for us in this: while we were still sinners, Christ died for us."

Meaning: The Gospel is not about us. While we were still dead in our sin, Christ died. It's about His sacrifice and the deep love of God. The life and death of Jesus is evidence of God's love for us.

4. Romans 10:9–10 NIV: "If you declare with your mouth, 'Jesus is Lord,' and believe in your heart that God raised Him from the dead, you will be saved. For it is with your heart that you believe and are justified, and it is with your mouth that you profess your faith and are saved."

Meaning: We are saved if we believe in and confess JESUS. There is no other way to salvation. Confessing out loud is proof of our faith. Believing in our hearts is that deep resolve to live what we preach. It is us internally declaring, "I'm all in." It justifies us in the eyes of God because of the blood of Jesus.

5. Romans 10:13 KJV: "For whosoever shall call upon the name of the Lord shall be saved."

Meaning: The Gospel is open to *all* who believe and call upon the name of Jesus.

Jesus did not die and rise again to make bad people good. He died and rose again to make dead people alive. He burst from the grave, with the heavens roaring, to give life and life abundantly to those buried in darkness. The invitation is clear, and it would be erroneous for me to breeze right past it.

So, if you are reading this and haven't committed your life to the Lord, take a deep breath and ask Jesus to make you alive. Believe in your heart that He truly is the Son of God, the Lord of all; believe that He took your sin and died in your place, rising again to defeat the grave, and confess out loud that you believe these truths and want to walk in His ways. Tell Him you give Him your life and take His upon you; His yoke is easy, and His burden is light. Your sins are forgiven; now, go and sin no more. Turn from your dead ways and walk in the light and life.

If you prayed that prayer, I want to be the first to welcome you into the family, dear friend; welcome to His family.

CHAPTER FOUR REFLECTION

Take 15-30 minutes to do this section; do not rush what the Lord is going to teach you during your time with Him. Before you jump to the questions, stop and ask God to speak to you. Ask Him to fill you with understanding and reveal His heart for you.

Connection to God is available to you through the death and resurrection of Jesus. Do you believe this? Have you given your life to Him? This is not a simple prayer; this is a holy exchange. Have you given Him everything? If yes, write out your salvation moment. If not, why haven't you yet?

If you have come to Jesus in the past because of fear of hell or because of what Jesus can bless you with, are you willing to repent and see the Gospel for what it is—a finished work of what Jesus did for you?

God desires all of you. There is no shame found in the finished work of the cross, only redemption and life. Are you holding any parts of yourself back from committing to God? If so, what and why?

Take 10 minutes to sit quietly and ask God to speak to you about this chapter. Believe that He will. Write down what you are asking Him and then write His reply.

CHAPTER FIVE

Born Again

Now there was a man of the Pharisees named Nicodemus, a leader of the Jews. He came to Jesus at night and said, "Rabbi, we know that You are a teacher who has come from God. For no one could perform the signs You are doing if God were not with him." Jesus replied, "Truly, truly, I tell you, no one can see the kingdom of God unless he is born again." "How can a man be born when he is old?" Nicodemus asked. "Can he enter his mother's womb a second time to be born? "Jesus answered, "Truly, truly, I tell you, no one can enter the kingdom of God unless he is born of water and the Spirit. Flesh is born of flesh, but spirit is born of the Spirit. Do not be amazed that I said, 'You must be born again.' The wind blows where it wishes. You hear its sound, but you do not know where it comes from or where it is going. So, it is with everyone born of the Spirit. (John 3:1–8 BSB)

When someone gives their life to Jesus, as we talked about in the previous chapter, they must be born again. And how does that happen, exactly? Well, we have already been born of flesh, through the womb of our mothers, but now we must be born of Spirit—born into the Kingdom of God, a brand-new world, in order to come alive to His call and purpose for our lives. To do so, we must be baptized, as we see through the following scriptures.

And Peter said to them, "Repent and be baptized every one of you in the name of Jesus Christ for the forgiveness of your sins, and you will receive the gift of the Holy Spirit." (Acts 2:38 ESV)

And now why do you wait? Rise and be baptized and wash away your sins, calling on his name. (Acts 22:16 ESV)

Whoever believes and is baptized will be saved, but whoever does not believe will be condemned. (Mark 16:16 ESV)

Of course, the list of scriptures talking about baptism goes on and on, but we'll stop there for now. It should be clear that baptism is crucial to the Gospel. Jesus even commands it in Matthew 28:19 ESV: "*Go therefore and make disciples of all nations, baptizing them in the name of the Father and of the Son and of the Holy Spirit.*" The act of water baptism isn't simply an outward sign or public display of faith, as some preach. That is part of it, but that isn't *why* Jesus tells us to do it.

There is profound depth to baptism—another mystery of the Kingdom we will not grasp in fullness until we are face to face with Him who raised us from the dead. But just because we can't fully comprehend what it means in the Spirit to be dunked under water and come back up again does not mean we should avoid it. If Jesus commanded it, we ought to do it. Obedience is key in the Kingdom, and 90 percent obedience is still disobedience. Still, He has great grace for us in the learning curve of surrender.

To better understand baptism, let's examine one of my favorite passages.

> *For Christ also suffered for sins once for all, the righteous for the unrighteous, to bring you to God. He was put to death in the body but made alive in the Spirit,*

> *in whom He also went and preached to the spirits in prison who disobeyed long ago when God waited patiently in the days of Noah while the ark was being built. In the ark a few people, only eight souls, were saved through water. And this water symbolizes the baptism that now saves you also—not the removal of dirt from the body, but the pledge off a clear conscience toward God—through the resurrection of Jesus Christ, who has gone into heaven and is at the right hand of God, with angels, authorities, and powers subject to Him. (1 Peter 3:18–22 BSB)*

God uses Noah's life as a symbol of the power and authority of baptism. I love to think about Bible stories through my own eyes, imagining what it would be like to be Noah and his family as they built the ark, watched God bring in the animals, and heard the rain pounding against the sides of the boat as the Lord shut the door. I cannot imagine what it would feel like to step off the ark when the earth was dry again and new life was beginning to grow. I want to explore the idea of baptism through the perspective of Noah and envision the reality that lay before him. (The following words are simply my interpretation of what might have been happening—a fictional retelling, if you will!)

* * *

Noah's eyes danced over the northern mountains, taking in their view. "Not a cloud in sight," he sighed. It had been years since the Lord spoke to him and told him to build. His heart had days when it grew weary from the scoffing of those he used to call friends. Lately, it was just him, his wife, the kids, and their families. Loneliness knocked at his door in moments like these, but he always reminded himself that the voice of his Lord far outweighed the logic of the world he lived in. Drunkenness, partying, sexual promiscuity, and gossip raged through his city, so it was best he didn't spend his days there anyway, for he knew his flesh had potential to be weak apart from God. It was better that he worked here day in and day out, building this boat for God only knew what. He was starting to get anxious, as they were only a few days from finishing it. "What's next, Lord?" he whispered.

His mind snapped back to reality when he heard his wife's voice echo through the hills as she approached him. "Noah! Noah, dinner's ready. The boys have come to join us," she sang out. Noah could sense the joy in her tone, and he could not help but smile. Her simple presence and steadfast faithfulness held him up on his weak days. God had blessed him with a wife who not only served him well but spoke her mind and loved the Lord above all else. “Coming, my love,” he responded as he grabbed his stick and started the walk back to camp. Naamah skipped over to join him. You’d never guess she was as old as she was. Noah couldn’t help but laugh at the sight of her, hair flying in the wind and her feet sliding over the stones. “Slow down, Naamah,” he grinned. “You aren’t 20 anymore.”

“I’m just happy,” she giggled. “The time is near, and you are almost done with the ark,” she smiled. Noah adored her. The world around them was deeply broken. People were killing each other, neglecting the Lord’s laws, and living solely for themselves, yet his wife still saw the good. It was times like these that Noah breathed out his abundant praise on the Lord. God was good, and even with all the unknowns of the future, Noah and his family could rest in His mercy. Naamah and Noah reached the camp and were greeted with huge smiles from their family. Peace. God had created a place for them.

Noah’s heart raced with excitement as he saw the clouds begin to swirl. God was moving, and it was now tangible. His smile quickly faded as he realized what that meant: rain was coming. The people were not prepared, and no one would survive. He frantically turned and quickly ran through the streets, shouting to the masses, "Turn your hearts to God! It is not too late. Let Him save you. There is room for you. There is a safe place for you!" The people laughed at him, and he heard one in the crowd huff, "Crazy old Noah's at it again."

"Look to the sky!" Noah shouted. "Don't you see? God's wrath is coming." But the people did not see. Their sin and selfishness blinded them from the truth. Noah's heart broke as they grabbed rocks and began to hurl them toward him. "Get out of here, you crazy old man! We will not tolerate this any longer. Get out, and do not come back, or we will kill you!" they screamed.

Noah ran for his life as tears poured down his cheeks. "Lord, save them," he choked.

"I am trying," God's voice rang out. "I have created a place for them; they need only come to Me."

It was so simple. Noah understood that. His family understood that. God had prepared Noah for what was coming and simply asked for humility, faithfulness, and trust in return. "Help them see," Noah begged. He stumbled back to the boat as the rain started to fall. There stood his wife, tears in her eyes. He could see the anxiety on her face, and he wrapped his arms around her.

"Noah," she cried, "what will become of us? Oh, I'm so scared."

Noah held her tight and gently tilted her chin upward. "Look to the sky, my love," he echoed. "The Lord said He would pour out His wrath on sin, and now He is, but He has provided a place for us in His great mercy. He is with us. His love endures forever. We are nothing but a speck of dust, and yet He thought of us. He loves us, Naamah. He truly loves us. He did not need to have us build a boat, but He did, and He gave us the perfect plans for it. And look, here comes His creation!" Noah exclaimed.

Naamah gasped as she took in the sight that lay before her: elephants, lions, deer, sheep, cows, dogs, and monkeys all walking together toward the boat in harmony. Two of each kind. "God is faithful," she whispered, "truly faithful. He has created a place for us all; we need only accept His grace and repent from our sins."

Noah's stomach twisted from the smell of the animals in the boat. The rain had finally ceased after 40 days and nights, but Noah and his family sat safely aboard, waiting for a sign that it was okay to leave. The raven he had sent never returned, and the dove came back empty the first time. Noah sent the dove again, and this time it returned with a branch. Life was beginning to return! It had been a long journey, and his family was ready to embark on this new adventure with the Lord. It was time—long overdue.

They were ready. God opened the doors, and the flood of light blinded Noah for a moment. He could hear the squeals of the animals filling the space as they poured out of the ark, and the joyful sobs of Naamah overwhelmed his heart. He felt her hand squeeze his as her voice floated through the air. "Open your eyes, Noah. You must see God's faithful promise."

He gasped as he took in the sight before him. Colors filled the sky in a magnificent arch. He had never seen anything like it before, and he sank to his knees in praise. The bow of wrath was pointed at the sky—a faithful promise from God that He had taken the sin of humanity upon Himself and would come to redeem all that had been broken by sin. Here, Noah would build an altar, a token of gratitude to the Lord, for He had created a place for them and kept them in the shelter of His wings. The voice of the Lord boomed across the mountains:

> *"I have set my rainbow in the clouds, and it will be the sign of the covenant between me and the earth. Whenever I bring clouds over the earth and the rainbow appears in the clouds, I will remember my covenant between me and you and all living creatures of every kind. Never again will the waters become a flood to destroy all life. Whenever the rainbow appears in the*

> *clouds, I will see it and remember the everlasting covenant between God and all living creatures of every kind on the earth." (Genesis 9: 13–16 NIV).*

It was as if God was making a promise to Noah: "Never again will I let floodwaters destroy all life. When I see the rainbow in the sky, I will always remember the promise that I have made to every living creature. The rainbow will be the sign of that solemn promise."

* * *

Across the sky, a colorful display of mercy was painted. This first rainbow was a sign of God's covenant that He would never flood the earth again. I have heard it said that it looks like a bow, pulled back and pointed at the heavens; a representation of God "taking the hit" for creation, saying, "I have turned the bow on myself; I will take your sin upon myself, bear your mistakes, and bring you new life. I will make a covenant, and I will not break it. I will redeem this in fullness one day." The significance of baptism is rooted in the story of the flood. It is more than just a symbol. Baptism is a graveyard. We emerge from the water into new life, leaving behind who we once were, dying to ourselves, and being raised again in His covenant. We receive a "birth certificate" from Heaven on our baptism day.

Now, instead of an ark, we see the fullness of redemption in Jesus Christ. We see the eternal boat of salvation that will bring us through *all* storms. There is another flood coming, metaphorical this time. God has promised never to flood the earth with water again. However, a flood of reality is coming. Humanity is on a highway to hell, headed toward the city of destruction, and the only exit route is the ark called Jesus. Baptism saves us because it is our commitment to join Christ, bowing in obedience to the Word of God, and it is our sign that we are entering the boat. It is our yes to God. We take His life upon us and walk out of the ark into the new, bright, fresh world He has prepared for us—the world that is His Kingdom.

Think about how the world appears to a new baby; it is loud, bright, and completely new. When a baby is born, it opens its mouth and cries. Breath fills its lungs as it inhales for the very first time. The baby relies solely on its mother for life and sustenance. Now, as we have grown, accepted Christ as our Savior, it is time to be born into His Kingdom. When we come to Jesus and give Him our lives, we take His life upon us and are born again. This is what baptism means. Baptism is the act of being fully immersed underwater, an act of "dying" to our old lives, and emerging from the water, breathing in a new reality of being washed clean by the blood of Jesus. We are tiny babies, catching our breath for the first time, eyes wide open to a brand-new world.

As a mother, giving birth changed me. There was a massive shift in my heart and life when I pushed my babies into this world. The day my body gave over to labor and delivered life was a day that would go down in history for me; it was a turning point. But for my children, that day was a wild awakening as well. It marked me, but it *transformed* them. They came wailing into a cold, scary, big world, and I was here. My arms were wide open, pulling them close and comforting them against my chest. This is the revelation of the Father; baptized into His Kingdom, we become family again, adopted and grafted in. We come as screaming, dependent children, needing the arms of our loving God to hold us, equip us, and teach us, and He is right there. Our birth into His family transforms us and marks Him. The heavens rejoice when a child comes home. We are born into a family.

It Doesn't End in the Water

When we come out of the water, born into the Kingdom of God, we need to be fed and sustained by the Word. We need people to teach us, Holy Spirit to bring us revelation, and time to grow. There is infinite beauty to being born into the Kingdom of God. I have seen people baptized and rise with healing, deliverance, and fresh revelation. I have also seen people rise with a new resolve to persevere for the rest of their lives.

Discipleship is crucial to this step of new life. When I lived in Bolivia, I had friends who taught me all about the country, history, culture, and formalities. I bartered with a private Spanish tutor to walk me through grammar and comprehension as I taught her English. I pushed myself out of my comfort zone and traveled around the city weekly by myself to learn the bus routes, roads, and locations of places I needed to get to. When I gave my life to Jesus, God prompted me to do this same thing. Throughout my faith walk, I have sought forth mentors, spiritual mothers and fathers, to teach me, guide me, and direct my eyes back to the Word when I grow weary.

When we are baptized, born into the family of God, it takes time to grow and learn. Don't rush these seasons of refining, studying, being mentored, and waiting on the

Lord. Give yourself grace as you are born again into the Kingdom of God, justified by the blood of Jesus, birthed through the water into new life, held by the arms of the Father, and sanctified by the Holy Spirit and fire. We are born into a family, but not just any family—we're born into *His* family.

If you have not yet been baptized, or if you were baptized as a baby or before you understood the significance of it, what are you waiting for? The time is now.

CHAPTER FIVE REFLECTION

Take 15-30 minutes to do this section; do not rush what the Lord is going to teach you during your time with Him. Before you jump to the questions, stop and ask God to speak to you. Ask Him to fill you with understanding and reveal His heart for you.

If you have given your life to Jesus, have you been baptized? If so, write out the story. If not, why not?

Baptism is our first act of faith in walking with God. If you were baptized as a baby or had water sprinkled on your head, are you willing to recommit to God through a full baptism?

____

____

____

____

____

____

Are you being discipled? Do you have mentors of the faith? If so, write their names down and thank them for pouring into you. If not, ask the Lord to send people to mentor you. If He brings someone to mind, call them now and ask if they would meet with you regularly to discuss the Bible.

____

____

____

____

Take 10 minutes to sit quietly and ask God to speak to you about this chapter. Believe that He will. Write down what you are asking Him and then write His reply.

CHAPTER SIX

Justification and Sanctification

Now that we have covered how to be born again into a new family, where do we go next? Let me "spiritual mother" you with some theology for a moment. There are two big, fancy terms thrown around in Christian culture quite often, and I find many new believers don't stop to understand their depth. We saw one of them listed in the Romans Road, and we will see the other one coming up here as we learn to walk out being a disciple of Christ. These two terms are *justification* and *sanctification*. If we, as believers, can gain a deeper understanding of how to apply these principles to daily life, then we will be better equipped to communicate the Gospel to those around us.

Often, I see these terms mixed up. *Justification*, according to the Merriam-Webster dictionary, is: "1a: the act or an instance of justifying something: vindication arguments offered in justification of their choice. 1b: an acceptable reason for doing something: something that justifies an act or way of behaving could provide no justification for his decision. 2: the act, process, or state of being justified by God."

Sanctification is defined by the Merriam-Webster dictionary as "1: an act of sanctifying. 2a: the state of being sanctified. 2b: the state of growing in divine grace as a result of Christian commitment after baptism or conversion."

In Romans, we see the belief in Jesus as the thing that declares us justified before God. This means that justification occurs instantaneously upon salvation. When we believe in our hearts and confess with our mouths that Christ is Lord, and that God raised him from the dead, we are justified before God. We see this in the story of the man on the cross next to Jesus.

> *One of the criminals who were hanged railed at him, saying, "Are you not the Christ? Save yourself and us!" But the other rebuked him, saying, "Do you not fear God, since you are under the same sentence of*

condemnation? And we indeed justly, for we are receiving the due reward of our deeds; but this man has done nothing wrong." And he said, "Jesus, remember me when you come into your kingdom." And he said to him, "Truly, I say to you, today you will be with me in paradise." (Luke 23:39–43 ESV)

The criminal acknowledges that Jesus is the Son of God, and Jesus says, "*Today* you will be with me." This man did not live a good life. He did nothing of value for the Kingdom of God except acknowledge Jesus as Savior. This simple revelation of Jesus as the Son of God warranted him a spot in paradise.

Our humanity does not like this. Pride can easily spring up and shout, "I lived my life perfectly and did all these good things for You! How does someone who murders and steals and curses You reap the same reward simply because they gave You their life on their deathbed?!" But you see, God shows no partiality. By earthly standards, His grace is scandalous. His Kingdom is for *all* who believe and receive, regardless of sin, background, race, color, lifestyle, and expectation, and the mercy of God covers a multitude of sins. I firmly believe that the man on the cross who acknowledged Jesus as Lord would have turned his whole life around, given the chance. Repentance and a genuine acceptance of Jesus lead to a complete turnaround in our actions; it changes our priorities. But our actions do not bring us into union with God.

Justification has absolutely nothing to do with us; it has everything to do with Jesus's standing before God. The way that we come to be justified is by belief in Jesus alone. That man on the cross died two deaths that day. He died a sinner's death unto himself and rose through Christ Jesus, meaning he *also* rose in salvation through Christ Jesus. After this, he died a human death on that cross, but what we know is that because of his redemption, he rose into eternal paradise that same day. This is the power of justification—it is an instantaneous process in which the blood of Jesus is poured out on us for our sins. It is an immediate redemption through the line of Jesus.

In the Old Testament, we see the story of the Israelites being held captive for generations as slaves to Pharaoh and the Egyptian army. But God had a plan to redeem and call people back to Himself. So, He appointed Moses and used him, along with his brother Aaron, as a mouthpiece and spokesperson to Pharaoh, calling forth the freedom of God's people. Pharaoh's heart was full of pride, and he refused to release the people. Even when God sent 10 plagues—10 different attempts at redemption for Pharaoh—he continued to refuse. So, the 10th plague was the final moment. God declared this plague would be an angel of death that would sweep through the city, killing the firstborn son of every family. This also applied to the Israelites.

The justice and mercy of God show no partiality; all have fallen short. Still, we see the great heart of God making a way out for anyone who believes and accepts. The firstborn sons of all people in the land would be killed because the judgment of God was being poured out on that land. What we find is that when the judgment of God is poured out on the land, the mercy of God is also poured out on the land for those who *listen.* Remember: Judgment and mercy always coincide.

God told the people to take a perfect lamb, sacrifice it, and use the blood as paint over the doorpost of their homes. When the angel of death would pass by these houses, he would pass over those that had the blood on the doorpost. (This is where the Jewish holiday of Passover originates.) In this story, we clearly see the mighty hand of God at work. Where there is judgment, there is also mercy; where there is demise, there is also salvation.

It was available to anyone who followed the voice of God and painted the blood on the doorpost. This is the same for you and me today. When we paint the blood of Jesus, figuratively, upon the doorpost of our hearts, we are justified—the angel of death passes over us. We are redeemed and restored into right standing for all eternity with God because of the sacrifice of Jesus.

Justification is a legal term. God is seen as the ultimate judge throughout the Bible, and He is also the lawmaker. He gives *and* enforces the law. Before Jesus, our standing before the judge was "guilty," not because of the nature of the judge, but because of the reality of the fall. Remember, Adam and Eve had covered themselves with fig leaves, but it wasn't enough to cover their shame. God made them a covering of skins, but that was not eternally sufficient for all of humanity. It was setting the stage for the ultimate lamb, the Lamb of God, who would take on the sins of the world. When Jesus came and redeemed us, giving His life in our place, the verdict changed.

Why was He born in a stable? Because He is a lamb. Why did He give up his will on earth to follow the Shepherd—even unto death? Because He is a lamb. Why did the Israelites paint the blood of a perfect lamb over their doorposts before the angel of death passed over them?

Because Jesus is the perfect Lamb, with perfect blood, that we "paint" over the doorposts of our souls.

Sanctification

Jesus is also seen as our advocate, standing before the judge and giving testimony of His covering. His blood speaks a better word, changing the sentence once and for all from "guilty" to "just as if I never did it." Completely justified. We are no longer seen by God as sinful, shame-filled, hidden-behind-fig-leaves people. He sees the blood of Jesus speaking holiness over us. We are seated in heavenly places, redeemed and restored to right standing with God. Holiness is our identity—it's what we live out of and *also* what we pursue. We are called holy by God because of Jesus alone, but now we have the honor of living out a pursuit of holiness, not from religious obligation, but from a deep, overwhelming love. This is *sanctification.*

Sanctification comes through walking with Holy Spirit. When Jesus ascended to Heaven after He rose from the grave, He declared that He would send His Spirit to teach, equip, and comfort. Now, when we accept Jesus, we receive access to Holy Spirit—the third person of the Trinity.

> *"If you love me, you will keep my commandments. And I will ask the Father, and he will give you another Helper, to be with you forever, even the Spirit of truth, whom the world cannot receive, because it neither sees him nor knows him. You know him, for he dwells with you and will be in you. I will not leave you as orphans; I will come to you. Yet a little while and the world will see me no more, but you will see me. Because I live, you also will live." (John 14:15–19 ESV)*

> *"These things I have spoken to you while I am still with you. But the Helper, the Holy Spirit, whom the Father will send in my name, he will teach you all things and bring to your remembrance all that I have said to you. Peace I leave with you; my peace I give to you. Not as the world gives do I give to you. Let not your hearts be troubled, neither let them be afraid." (John 14: 25–27 ESV)*

The Holy Spirit works to reveal the mysteries of the Kingdom and guides us to become more like God. We will never *be* God, nor will we ever be perfect, but we can learn to walk in righteousness and honor the Lord in all things. Sanctification is a continuous process of moving from glory to glory; of becoming more and more like Jesus. It is refinement. I like to compare this process to my gardens. Every spring, when I start preparing my flowerbeds, the Lord begins to speak to me about sanctification. First, there is pruning and weed pulling to do. There is leaf removal from past seasons, fresh mulch to spread on the ground, and new plants to replace the dead ones.

Similarly, in our hearts, when the Lord begins His work of sanctification, there are things that need to be removed. There is pruning that needs to happen, which can be quite painful. Old leaves from past seasons need to be washed away, revealing the tender soil beneath. Then, we must apply the Lord's balm to that fresh soil to protect it from harsh winds that life may bring. Sometimes, plants must be uprooted and replanted in different beds for their safety. Other times, we need to plant new ones because the old plants have died. There are seasons for rest and seasons for harvest. This is a continuous process of sanctification and growth with the Holy Spirit.

We will not reach the end of this process until we are in eternity with the Lord. For the rest of our days here on earth, we will need Holy Spirit to work in our hearts for sanctification. I absolutely love this process with Him. I know that my life before God is justified, but I also know that my life before man needs to be refined if I want to lead people to the King of kings. I want to spend my days working to look more and more like Him. If I want to lead people to the Fisher of men, I need to learn how to be a better fisherman, and I want to learn from the Fisher of all men first. If I want to lead people to the Shepherd Himself, I need to learn how to better feed the sheep from the great Shepherd Himself. Sanctification is a gift and a privilege that we have when we walk with Christ. It is an outpouring of surrender and love, but it is also an infilling of power and an advancing of the Kingdom.

In the wise words of Spider-Man, "With great power comes great responsibility." When we have the Kingdom of Heaven inside us, bursting at the seams, we bear an incredible responsibility to steward it well. The greatest tool we have for sharing the Gospel is our conduct and character. How you carry yourself and treat others speaks volumes about who you follow. How you carry yourself confirms the message you preach.

Sanctification is a stewardship of the Kingdom within us. We may be justified, but are we being sanctified? Are we allowing God to uproot things that need to be uprooted? Are we allowing God to move mountains in us before asking Him to move mountains through us? I have come to deeply realize that God cares more about my character than He does my ministry. My life is the very first ministry people encounter, long before I even open my mouth. If my life does not reflect the Kingdom of Heaven, I am doing a great disservice to the glory of God. Sanctification is an honor. It is a privilege and a responsibility that we should not take lightly.

CHAPTER SIX REFLECTION

Take 15-30 minutes to do this section; do not rush what the Lord is going to teach you during your time with Him. Before you jump to the questions, stop and ask God to speak to you. Ask Him to fill you with understanding and reveal His heart for you.

What is one area you need Holy Spirit to sanctify in you?

Are you willing to surrender that area to Him today? What does that surrender look like for you?

____

____

____

____

____

____

Are you trying to justify why you belong in Heaven? Example: "I am a good person, and I did good things, so I belong there." Do you believe and understand that the justification of your place before God is only given through the sacrifice of Jesus?

____

____

____

____

____

____

Take 10 minutes to sit quietly and ask God to speak to you about this chapter. Believe that He will. Write down what you are asking Him and then write His reply.

CHAPTER SEVEN

Pure in Heart

Blessed are the pure in heart, for they shall see God. (Matthew 5:8 ESV)

The beautiful work of sanctification is a deep gift, and it is one that holds eternal value and perspective, but it also holds great weight of glory for *now*. One of the most important parts of the sanctification process is growing in purity.

This may not be the first chapter many people would think to write in a book about the Gospel, but it is the one I knew I needed to include before I even started Chapter One. The Bible makes it clear that purity is crucial to seeing God. Now, let me be clear: When I talk about purity, I'm not just referring to sexual purity, as some might assume. I'm talking about lifestyle purity that stems from soul purity, which involves your mind, will, and emotions. It's about aligning your heart with the Kingdom perspective and living from that place. Salvation through Jesus is the *only* gate that gets us into the Kingdom and the Kingdom into us. There are areas of the Kingdom that we have the privilege to explore as we align our hearts with His. Purity is one of these; it's like gravel pathways running through the hidden passages of His Kingdom. Few walk them, but those who do will taste the beauty of His glory.

But purity is not something we can perfect. We are not "better" people or more "high and mighty" simply because we live lives of purity, but we do gain a clearer perspective, and the weight of glory will rest on us in great measure when we pursue what matters to Him. And let me tell you, friend, purity matters to Him.

Lately, I've noticed a trend in church culture that deeply concerns me, and it's not a new one. It's a pattern we see throughout the Bible, and it's still happening today: compromise. We often live for ourselves from Monday to Friday, and then on Saturday or Sunday—depending on the culture and when you observe the Sabbath—we live for God. People go out, get drunk, sleep around, get into fights, watch porn, lie, and cheat on Saturday, then put on a perfect face for church on Sunday. Many also appear to live "perfect" lives outwardly but are truly dead inside, asleep to the things that matter to God. In the Bible, Jesus rebukes the Pharisees for this, saying, *"Woe to you, scribes and Pharisees, hypocrites! For you are like whitewashed tombs, which outwardly appear beautiful, but within are full of dead people's bones and all uncleanness"* (Matthew 23:27 ESV).

"Blessed are the pure in heart, for they shall see God"—this refers to those truly pure in heart, not just those who are merely cleaned up on the outside. The beauty of having a pure heart is that the outside reflects what's inside. Life flows from within, full of deep beauty and purpose. But if we're only concerned about our purity on the outside, the heart itself may be dead, and that will show in our character, attitude, and compromises.

Purity of heart isn't preached enough, in my opinion. I believe this is because it's not a flashy message. If I wanted to gather a bigger following and ensure this book was well-received, I would never write about being pure in heart and avoiding compromise. I would write about exciting things like the Lord's blessings on your life when you accept Him. I would write about the prosperity gospel—how we receive Christ in order to receive what He has for us. I would write about the gifts of the Spirit without requiring fruit. I would share stories of miracles, signs, and wonders, but I would never highlight what happens when we sacrifice our character simply to see the gifts of God on this earth.

The gifts of God, without the fruit of God, cause an explosion of fire that dwindles out swiftly. If we want to see a lasting move of God, we must care as much about fruit as we do about gifts. We must be willing to examine the compromises in our own character and seek the Lord in every area. We must have holy reverence and fear of the Lord. We should be willing to say, "God, search me and know me; weed out the things in my life that need to go." We need to say no to sin and compromise. Some things may not be wrong or sinful, but they are not beneficial. We must be willing to sacrifice those things for that which is greater and lasting. This is an eternal perspective.

When I think about purity, I think about alignment. It is not mainly about living a pure and good life to see more of God; rather, it is about aligning our hearts with God and allowing our actions to reflect our true intentions. If my heart is rooted in the foundation of Jesus

Christ, my fruit will be the fruit of the Spirit. If my heart is rooted in compromise, impurity, or selfish ambition, my fruit will show that. As Dan Mohler often preaches, "If you squeeze an orange, you expect orange juice. If you squeeze a Christian, you should expect Jesus." The fruit of a person's life always shows evidence of the root in their life. In the words of one of my mentors, Sandy, "The fruit always reveals the root."

Seek His Heart, Not Just His Hand

In assessing our hearts for purity and alignment with God, we must check our motivations. Are they rooted in honoring Him through serving Him, or are our motives found in receiving from Him? We must ask the question: "Do I love the promise more than the Promise Keeper?"

But we aren't the only ones who have asked this question. In Genesis 17, Abraham is growing in age and has no direct heir to carry on his name. God promises his wife Sarah that she will have a son named Isaac, and she does. God remains faithful to His promises and makes a covenant with Abraham, pledging to continue to be loyal to his lineage. Then, in a surprising turn, in Genesis 22, God asks Abraham to take Isaac up the mountain, build an altar, and sacrifice him on it. Phew. This doesn't sound like the God of love and mercy that most of us know and love, so how could He ask this of Abraham?

What we find happening here is God asking Abraham through deed and obedience, "Do you love Me, the Promise Maker, more than you love Isaac, the result of My promise?" Abraham, though distraught, follows through in faith and obedience to God, prepared to sacrifice Isaac. Just before he does, God stops him and reveals a ram in the bushes, meant for the sacrifice. Abraham rejoices, and together with him, Isaac sacrifices the ram as an offering unto God.

The imagery and symbolism here are rich. What we see is God asking for faith *in Him* rather than just trusting in a promise, and He reveals that the plan is not about redemption through our efforts, but provision through His. The sacrifice of Jesus was established before God ever asks us to give our lives. However, to access the ram, which is the blood poured out from Jesus, we must have faith to figuratively lay ourselves on the altar. We must be willing to surrender our lives, to not love them so much that we refuse to die—literally if the Gospel requires it, and figuratively as we die to self and live from pure alignment with the Kingdom. Do you love the promise more than you love the Promise Maker? Do you love the gifts more than you love the Giver? Do you love what He does for you more than you desire to walk in purity? Do you love the Gospel for what it gives more than what you're willing to sacrifice for it? Do you love Him, or do you simply need Him? What is your motivation and intent?

There are hundreds of phenomenally gifted men and women of God out there, moving in signs and wonders, witnessing miracles, and walking in a great measure of anointing. Some are doing deep character work, standing firm, and refusing to compromise their conscience. Yet, some of these gifted men and women are operating out of selfish ambition and poor intent. It would be a mistake for me to overlook the fact that many great teachers, leaders, and pastors have fallen into sin and compromise over the years, or that many people have been hurt by such leaders. It would also be wrong for me to say all leaders are like this and that we should fear gifting and calling. What we *should* fear is a lack of the fear of the Lord and our alignment with Him. What we should fear is a lack of His voice guiding us. What we should fear is being unable to hear that still, small, gentle voice because we have violated our conscience too many times. What we should fear is allowing our character, integrity, and purity to be compromised so much so that we end up missing the Lord.

I weep as I write this. I never want to reach a point where I have violated the Word and voice of God so many times that I cannot hear Him clearly anymore. I never want to violate my conscience by seeing through clouded lenses of pride and desire, and in turn miss what God is doing on this earth. Have Your way, Lord Jesus! Refine us; purify Your bride, the Church. May You find us pure and set apart for You when You return.

Living out the Gospel is not about seeing a great move of God; it's about knowing the greatness of Him who is, was, and always will be. It is about walking with Him day in and day out. It's about seeing and knowing Him personally. The hand of God can never outrun the heart of God, and the heart of God can never outrun the face of God.

I want to take a moment to talk about Moses, who witnessed incredible acts of the hand of God. He encountered God in a burning bush and heard the booming voice of the Most High speak through that fire. He saw the 10 plagues poured out from the heavens. He watched as his people trembled in fear while being cornered by Pharaoh's army on one side and the Red Sea on the other. Moses raised his staff and watched the power of God split the water into two. He saw the mighty hand of God send bread from Heaven and bring forth water from the rock. This man had *seen* glory. And yet, we still find him ascending the hill of the Lord, asking God to reveal His glory. As I prayed through this one evening, the Lord began stirring my spirit and said, "Marissa, you misunderstand My glory. My hand is not My glory; My face is."

If we are simply seeking the hand of God, our heart's intent is not pure. If we only seek His hand for signs, wonders, and miracles, but never truly gaze upon His face, asking to revel in His glorious nature, we miss something essential to the Gospel. On the other hand, if we are only seeking His heart and running scared of His hand, His correction, and His power, we miss another important aspect. This message is not about *seeing* what He can do and will do. It is about *knowing* who He is and what He has done. Again, His hand cannot outrun His face, which cannot outrun His heart. To know Him is to see Him, and to see Him is to know Him.

CHAPTER SEVEN REFLECTION

Take 15-30 minutes to do this section; do not rush what the Lord is going to teach you during your time with Him. Before you jump to the questions, stop and ask God to speak to you. Ask Him to fill you with understanding and reveal His heart for you.

Examine your heart. Did something convict you in this past chapter? Is there an area you have not been walking in purity of heart that you need to surrender to the Lord?

____

____

____

____

____

____

Do you come to God simply to thank Him for all He has done and for who He is, or are you always coming to Him for what He can give you and all the problems you need Him to fix? If you are always asking for more, stop and write all you are thankful for that He has done.

Which fruit of the Spirit—love, joy, peace, patience, kindness, goodness, gentleness, faithfulness, and self-control—do you need more of in your life? Ask Holy Spirit to grow this in you.

Take 10 minutes to sit quietly and ask God to speak to you about this chapter. Believe that He will. Write down what you are asking Him and then write His reply.

CHAPTER EIGHT

Holy Spirit

"Nevertheless, I tell you the truth: it is to your advantage that I go away, for if I do not go away, the Helper will not come to you. But if I go, I will send him to you." (John 16:7 ESV)

Because our identity has been justified, covered by the blood of Jesus, we stand before God in the Kingdom of Heaven as if we never sinned. We can run boldly into the throne room, falling at His feet and embracing Him who gave us life. We have a place in His Kingdom. It might seem blasphemous to a religious spirit to talk about holiness, but it is now the birthright of every born-again believer. We have been made new in Christ. The blood of the Lamb is painted on the doorpost of our lives, marking us as redeemed and made new. Holiness is our identity, but the flesh can still be weak.

Living from holiness is difficult but is a deep joy as well. We often need to renew our minds in this practice. Praise the Lord for Holy Spirit: our best friend, teacher, and guide. There is a Helper—one who has been hovering over the waters from the beginning, moving on the very word of God (Genesis 1). The Holy Spirit moves on God's word, causing it to become action. There is incredible power in partnering with what God is doing, but even greater power in partnering with *whom* Jesus has sent. The Helper, also called Holy Spirit, is for the equipping, teaching, comforting, and helping of the body of Christ. He provides deep revelation about Jesus to the hearts of people, revealing the mysteries of the Kingdom in partnership with the Father and the Son. We cannot neglect Him.

I grew up in a culture that talked about Holy Spirit as one who convicts us of sin but little else. When I encountered Him as a Person at age 17, it changed everything for me. I realized I had limited Him by fearing the unknown. As I have grown in God, I have also seen the opposite—cultures and people that follow Holy Spirit for what He can give, but miss the person Holy Spirit reveals—Jesus, the Word of God. I am deeply grateful to have grown up in a church and culture rooted in the Word, knowing and preaching it as true, infallible, and spoken by God, recorded through man. I am also forever indebted to the Lord for opening my eyes to Holy Spirit and His tangible presence. Meeting Him filled me with fire and set me on a two-day journey of devouring my Bible—reading the New Testament all night as I lay awake, fully enraptured by His revelation. His Word prompted me to encounter His Spirit, and His Spirit pushed me to know His Word in greater measure. We cannot have Spirit without Word, and we cannot have Word without Spirit.

The working of Holy Spirit in signs and wonders is confirmation of the word that is preached, as we can see in the following scriptures:

> *And God confirmed the message by giving signs and wonders and various miracles and gifts of the Holy Spirit whenever he chose.* (Hebrews 2:4 NLT)

> *And they went out and preached everywhere, while the Lord worked with them and confirmed the message by accompanying signs.* (Mark 16:20 ESV)

There is great power in testimony and theology united as one. It is one thing for me to say Jesus is real; it is another for Him to show up and confirm the message that was just spoken. For all my days, I plan to dig into the Bible, asking the person of Holy Spirit to reveal its deep truths to my heart. His Spirit accompanies those who believe, as a gift to reveal His Kingdom first to the believer, and then to those around them.

> *He said to them, "Go into all the world and preach the gospel to all creation. Whoever believes and is baptized will be saved, but whoever does not believe will be condemned. And these signs will accompany those who believe: In my name they will drive out demons; they will speak in new tongues; they will pick up snakes with their hands; and when they drink deadly poison, it will not hurt them at all; they will place their hands on sick people, and they will get well." (Mark 16: 15–18 NIV)*

The promise of Holy Spirit is not just for the one who receives Him; He is a gift meant to be shared. He is a person meant to be introduced—a person who reveals Christ. He is one who sanctifies us so we look more and more like Jesus in our actions and thoughts. Much of this personal relationship revolves around submission. My soul—my mind, will, and emotions—is fickle.

It frequently leads me astray, keeping my eyes on myself and off my God, who can do more than I can ask, think, or imagine. Every situation, moment, and thought is an opportunity to submit my mind, will, and emotions either to the flesh, which is pride, or to the Spirit, which is truth. It is only through His power that I can do this.

I am not strong enough to walk in holiness without the help of the Spirit, nor am I meant to be. After all, if we could save ourselves, there would be no need for Jesus, and certainly no need for His Spirit. But we needed a Savior, perfect and Holy, the only one who could bridge the gap. Jesus lived a perfect life. He is the only one who could hold the hand of God because He was sinless—there was no pride in Him. And He was the only one who could hold the hand of man, because He became man Himself. He reached out, took the hand of man, and connected it back to the hand of God.

We needed Him. Humanity was quickly heading down the path that leads to destruction, and without intervention, hell is where we would have ended up. But the heavens roared, and intervention came in the form of a child named Jesus. After He died and rose again, He said that it was better for Him to go so that the Helper may come. I do not know about you, but I would have loved for Jesus to stay. I would love to spend my days sitting with Him, learning and growing at His feet. So, there must be a reason He said it was better for us to have His Spirit, right?

The Bible says that the Spirit dwells in the hearts of all who believe and receive Jesus and is the revealer of all things. He is a living, active being. He is a teacher, an equipper, and a friend. I cannot do ministry without Him. I cannot read my Word and comprehend it without Him. I cannot love my family well without Him. Goodness gracious, I cannot even go to the store without Him. I *need* Him. He has become my best friend. I take time each day to ask Him what He is doing. "What are You trying to reveal to me today? What do You see?"

We spend so much time trying to figure out how to do church, ministry, and life, or how to serve those around us. What do they need? What will they respond best to? What moves their hearts? We even try to figure out how to do it best for God. What does He need us to do? But have we stopped long enough to ask God what He wants, what moves His heart? Have we stopped to say good morning to Holy Spirit, to thank Him for the fruit He is growing in our lives, and to ask Him to confirm the word we speak today through His actions? Have we stopped to thank Him? He is not asking for people who only come to Him for what He can give. He is looking for servants who love Him and choose to give it all for His Kingdom to come.

Partnership with the family of the Trinity is an honor. I plan to spend my days learning to hear Him in greater measure, responding quickly to that voice, and repenting often for my failures. I plan to learn to love like Him, allowing His signs to confirm my message, and pouring out my praise on Him who is worthy of all glory. There is power in walking with Him. May the heavens rejoice as we share our stories of His faithfulness. May Holy Spirit be evident in our lives.

CHAPTER EIGHT REFLECTION

Take 15-30 minutes to do this section; do not rush what the Lord is going to teach you during your time with Him. Before you jump to the questions, stop and ask God to speak to you. Ask Him to fill you with understanding and reveal His heart for you.

All believers have Holy Spirit when they give their lives to Jesus. But there is an active filling of Holy Spirit that happens when we ask. Have you been baptized by the Spirit, filled with His power, gifts, and fruit? If so, write about it here. If not, do you want Him in greater measure? Tell Him. Then, pause and with open arms, ask Him to fill you.

Is there an area of your soul—mind, will, and emotions—that you need Holy Spirit's help with? Write it out and give it to Him today. Ask Him to lead you.

Have you shared your testimony before? Write out your story here. Who were you before you surrendered to God and were filled with Holy Spirit? How did you meet Jesus? Challenge yourself to share this with one person this week.

Take 10 minutes to sit quietly and ask God to speak to you about this chapter. Believe that He will. Write down what you are asking Him, and then write His reply.

CHAPTER NINE

Kingdom Culture

"I pledge allegiance to the flag of the United States of America..."

As an American citizen, I've often heard this. In fact, many schools recite it daily, and many other countries do the same. We pledge our allegiance to our nation and declare that we will love her, care for her, and protect her for all our days. When I think about it, I am reminded of how important allegiances really are. We are all part of earthly kingdoms, and honoring that kingdom is vital for survival and growth. We invest where we are planted, aiming to nurture and expand that culture. Now, how does this imagery relate to Kingdom culture as we talk about walking with God?

For all of history, we have seen kings, dictators, presidents, and emperors rise to power for a season and then fall. But we see in the Bible that a Kingdom has been established—one that will last the test of time and, one day, at the return of Christ, will reign for the rest of eternity. God is named the King of all kings who resides over the Kingdom of God, and those who believe that Jesus is the Savior are part of this Kingdom.

I love to think about this from the perspective of a princess. My Father, the King, has given me a cloak of identity; He has clothed me with the emblem of His Kingdom, forever marking me as His daughter and giving me a place called Home. But this cloak of identity also gives me authority. As His daughter, dressed in the righteousness of Jesus, I have authority. Darkness sees this cloak and flees. This cloak is the blood of the Lamb that speaks a better word over us. It has nothing to do with us, and yet our King places it on our shoulders and calls us His. He first pledged His love to us. We now have the honor of pledging our love and allegiance to Him and His Kingdom for the rest of our days. But in the Kingdom of God, pledging our allegiance to Him requires full submission. To walk out the Gospel here on earth, we must know the Kingdom we represent and be fully committed to following in the ways of Jesus.

It's important to understand that acknowledgment, acceptance, and submission are all very different terms. We can acknowledge that God exists without accepting or submitting to Him. Satan and demons acknowledge Jesus as Lord; they tremble in His presence. However, they are not part of His Kingdom. The Gospel is not merely about recognizing the Truth; it's about accepting Jesus and submitting to Him as King. He is our Savior *and* our Lord. We give Him everything. Many people accept that there is a God, and some even believe in Jesus, but they do not want to be part of His Kingdom or walk in His ways. I can acknowledge Him as King, but still refuse to let Him place His cloak of identity and authority on my shoulders. Or I can bow before Him in submission, allowing Him to clothe me in righteousness. To truly live from a place of Kingdom culture, complete submission is necessary. We pledge our allegiance wholeheartedly to the King of kings; we follow Him regardless of the cost, even if it leads to death.

Now, I don't know about you, but I am unwilling to die for someone I do not know and for something I do not 100 percent believe in. The cost of following the Gospel is our very lives—in life and in death, we give ourselves to His purposes and glory. But, in order to give ourselves to Him, we must know Him. So, how do we know this King we are following? Who draws the standards for the Kingdom we are expanding with dominion and authority? Let's dig into this.

There is a key difference between knowing God and *knowing* God. The English language does not hold great terminology for this, but Spanish does. In Spanish, there are two words that both mean "to know": *saber* and *conocer*. *Saber* means to literally know a fact. I know (saber) that Harrisburg is the capital of Pennsylvania. I know (saber) that most people in Bolivia speak Spanish. *Conocer* means to personally be familiar or acquainted with. I know (conocer) Bolivia; I lived there for a season of my life. I know (conocer) my son; I gave birth to him. We must *conocer* the Lord and His Kingdom. We cannot be people who just *saber* the things of God.

It is important to know facts, study theology, and gain historical knowledge to better understand the culture and context in which the Bible was written, as well as the Kingdom we are now part of. But we cannot simply read and study facts without knowing the Person behind them, or else we are just glorified scholars of history. To love Him is to know Him, and to know Him is to love Him. The best way to understand the things of the

Kingdom is to ask Holy Spirit to reveal Jesus to us. Only through the unveiling of Jesus can we understand the Kingdom of Heaven.

Jesus says in John 17:16 ESV, *"They are not of the world, just as I am not of the world."* We live in this world to reveal the Kingdom of Heaven in alignment with what Jesus has said, and we must know our King in order to share our King. We must live *from* knowledge rooted in relationship; we do not seek knowledge apart from relationship. We have the privilege of knowing our King personally, deeply, and daily. What an absolute honor. Our authority to expand the Kingdom here on earth *only comes* from a relationship with Jesus because *He alone* carries all authority. He sets the standard. He is the cloak we wear. He is the authority.

A Kingdom of Relationship

Many didn't receive Jesus as He walked the earth, and His Kingdom continues to be rejected today. When we look at our world, it is quite clear that the Kingdom of Heaven contradicts much of what is believed and received in culture, creating conflict. But what does Kingdom culture even look like, practically speaking?

Living from a Kingdom culture means that, first and foremost, we, as His followers, focus on God and what matters to His heart. We stand by and defend Truth despite what culture says. That said, we shouldn't be confronting others with theology without love. Instead, our words must be bathed in love and justice because God Himself is love. Through relationship, we come to know God deeply, and from that relationship, we make God known radically. We put Him above all else. When we truly believe this Gospel, it transforms how we think and act.

If you're preaching more than you're praying, you're missing the core of the Kingdom. It's a Kingdom of relationship with the King, not promoting Him outside of His presence. It is a Kingdom of fruit: love, joy, peace, patience, and self-control, to name a few.

Putting God's Kingdom before earthly kingdoms may seem strange to those who don't know the Lord; in fact, it is a radical idea. My political, theological, and cultural views are not based on how I was raised, where I reside, or the leaders I follow. Those things all play a role in how I see the world and the thought processes I have, but they are not the laws written on my heart. My heart's desire and culture are rooted in the person of Jesus, the finished work of the cross, and the Kingdom He has established. This Kingdom is eternal, and we are already living in it, even if we cannot see it with earthly eyes.

One day, Jesus will return and, in fullness, establish His Kingdom here. The book of Revelation speaks on this extensively. God is preparing a New Jerusalem that will come and rest on a new earth that is perfectly redeemed, and it will be ruled by Jesus Christ. The Father Himself will come and rest here, walking again with humankind for all of eternity.

If you have accepted Jesus as your Savior *and* Lord and are committed to following Him in every area, you are a member of His Kingdom, cloaked with identity and authority. You, my friend, are not just saved from hell; you are saved into God's eternal family, into relationship with the King. Live from this truth. His Word trumps any words of this world, and any lies you have believed before. His voice holds the final authority. You don't need to fear the things of this world or what is to come; you are grafted in and adopted as a son or daughter into His Kingdom, clothed in righteousness by the King of all kings. For now, we see only in part, but one day, perfection will come, and we will see in full.

Spend time each day getting to know your King. Friendship with God is available to you through the cloak of the blood of Jesus. The ability to "walk in the cool of the garden" with Him is ours once again. This Kingdom is not about expansion apart from relationship. It is about knowing God, deeply and personally, and from that place, making Him known, radically and intimately.

CHAPTER NINE REFLECTION

Take 15-30 minutes to do this section; do not rush what the Lord is going to teach you during your time with Him. Before you jump to the questions, stop and ask God to speak to you. Ask Him to fill you with understanding and reveal His heart for you.

Have you thought about Kingdom reality and culture before? If so, did this confirm much of what you know? If not, did this chapter open your eyes to any new truths?

Are there areas of life that you are living in this earthly culture that God is highlighting you need to surrender in order to walk in His Kingdom reality?

Reflect: are you sharing your faith with love, deeply desiring all to awaken to a revelation that they too may know God, or are you sharing your faith with aggression and frustration? This is a Kingdom of relationship first. How are you treating other people? Be honest with yourself here.

Take 10 minutes to sit quietly and ask God to speak to you about this chapter. Believe that He will. Write down what you are asking Him and then write His reply.

CONCLUSION

In the beginning, God created the heavens and the earth. The earth was without form and void, and darkness was over the face of the deep. And the Spirit of God was hovering over the face of the waters. God said, "Let there be light," and there was light (Genesis 1:1–3 ESV).

God brought light to the dark places, gave form to the emptiness, and granted understanding to veiled hearts through the revelation of Christ Jesus our Lord. "Let there be light." It is my deepest prayer that light poured into the dark places of your soul and heart as you read these chapters. I can say with a deep, holy unction, there is no life apart from Jesus. He is the way, the truth, and the life. Life stems from relationship with Him alone.

Light came through the very voice of God, and it continues to come that way day in and day out in our hearts. *You can hear Him now*. You are connected to His voice once again, walking in the cool of the Garden with God Himself because of the sacrifice of the Lamb, the perfect eternal covering for sin. Light came through the blood of Jesus, poured out on your behalf.

You can also *see with an unveiled heart* because Jesus has advocated on your behalf, giving Himself as your redeemer, forever drawing you into relationship with the Trinity. Light came through the gift of Holy Spirit, who speaks freedom and reveals *all* mysteries of the Gospel.

Lastly, you can *receive* because God is a good Father who gives good gifts to His children. You have access to His gifts and fruit because of Jesus and the work He has done. This fruit comes through relationship, submission, and attachment to the vine.

> *"I am the vine; you are the branches. If you remain in me and I in you, you will bear much fruit; apart from me you can do nothing" (John 15:5 NIV).*

We are grafted in, chosen, and redeemed, connected to the vine of life, which is Jesus. It is now time to make Him known—to bear much fruit. Go and reveal Christ to those around you. Go and make God known. Never stop getting to know Him. Never stop growing in relationship with the King of kings. The unveiled Gospel is yours. Go.

> *[Jesus] said to them, "Go into all the world and preach the gospel to all creation," (Mark 16:15 NIV).*

Father, I thank You for the work You have done through the pages of this story—Your story—and I bless the revelation You have deposited into hearts and minds. I thank You that this is a season of great awakening, revelation, and relationship with the King of kings. I thank You that the Gospel is a gift meant to be known and shared, unveiled and released to *all the world.* I thank You for who You are, for the sacrifice of Jesus, and for the love You so deeply have for us. We receive all You have given us and asked us to step into, and we say YES with boldness and a fire in our bellies. We will go anywhere. We will do anything for the sake of Your Kingdom come and Your will be done here on earth as it is in Heaven. We say yes to You today, Jesus. We love You. We honor You. We glorify You. Make Your glory known here.

Love,

Your children who see with unveiled faces *all* that You have set before us. Amen.

ACKNOWLEDGMENTS

To my best friend, champion, biggest supporter, love, and partner, my husband, Sean: thank you. You've made this book possible, and you have helped shape much of the way I see God. You have faith unlike anyone I have met, and you know the Lord deeply. I learn daily from you. I am eternally grateful for the gift of your love and leadership. I honor you and love you always.

To my children, the loves of my life, thank you. You three have revealed the love of Father God to me in ways I could never have imagined, and I am deeply blessed to be your mama. Your joy is contagious, and you radiate the love of Christ in your laughter, questions, and learning. You are the greatest reward I have the honor of stewarding, discipling, and loving. I love you forever.

To my mom and dad, thank you. You revealed Christ to me and raised me to know the Word, walking in the ways of God. There will never be words for how grateful I am to have been raised by you. Well done good and faithful servants of the Lord. I love you both dearly.

To my editor, Katie Rios, thank you for a job well done—for shaping this book and honoring Holy Spirit in every word, edit, and conversation. You are a light shining bright, and I am blessed by your work and friendship. May you never lack anything as you pursue His heart all your days.

To my publisher, Tall Pine, thank you. From the very first email, you have been a joy to work with. Thank you for loving the Lord above all else and thank you for championing the work of God in authors. May His light shine upon you in greater measure as you continue to honor Him.

To all those who have gone before me, paving the way of discipleship in my heart—my mothers and fathers of the faith—thank you. There are too many names to write but thank you all for your yes to the Lord which in turn has helped shape my yes to Him. I am deeply grateful for each of you and the way God has used you to refine, correct, sharpen, and shape me.

And lastly, to all who come after me, listening to my words and learning from seats at my table, thank you. You have revealed the power of unveiling Jesus. You have shaped me as a servant of God, and I am eternally grateful that God has allowed me the honor of teaching and equipping you. May you in turn be bold and fruitful, teaching those around you the power of the Gospel. Thank you for *your* yes to Him.

MARISSA BUSBY is a worshiper of Jesus with a heart for discipleship in south eastern Pennsylvania. She has a desire to see people truly know God and radically make Him known. She has been in ministry for twelve years-since the age of 18. In her personal time, she is a wife and mother, and much of her discipleship stems from how she raises her kids. She also has a passion for coaching CrossFit and teaching people they can do all things through Christ who strengthens them.

www.ingramcontent.com/pod-product-compliance
Lightning Source LLC
LaVergne TN
LVHW010948110826
845149LV00015B/3264
* 9 7 8 1 9 6 7 2 6 2 4 4 1 *